# Surviving The Galveston Hurricane

By Jo Cleland

Illustrated By Pete McDonnell

ROURKE PUBLISHING

Vero Beach, Florida 32964

www.rourkepublishing.com

Edited by Meg Greve
Illustrated by Pete McDonnell
Art Direction and Page Layout by Renee Brady

**Library of Congress Cataloging-in-Publication Data**

Cleland, Joann.
 Surviving the Galveston hurricane / Jo Cleland.
     p. cm. --  (Eye on history graphic illustrated)
 Includes bibliographical references and index.
 ISBN 978-1-60694-438-7 (alk. paper)
 ISBN 978-1-60694-547-6 (soft cover)
 1.  Galveston (Tex.)--History--20th century--Juvenile literature. 2.  Hurricanes--Texas--Galveston--History--20th century--Juvenile literature. 3.  Floods--Texas--Galveston--History--20th century--Juvenile literature. 4.  Graphic novels.  I. Title.
 F394.G2C55 2010
 976.4'139061--dc22
                                              2009020499

Printed in the U.S.A.
CG/CG

www.rourkepublishing.com - rourke@rourkepublishing.com
Post Office Box 643328  Vero Beach, Florida 32964

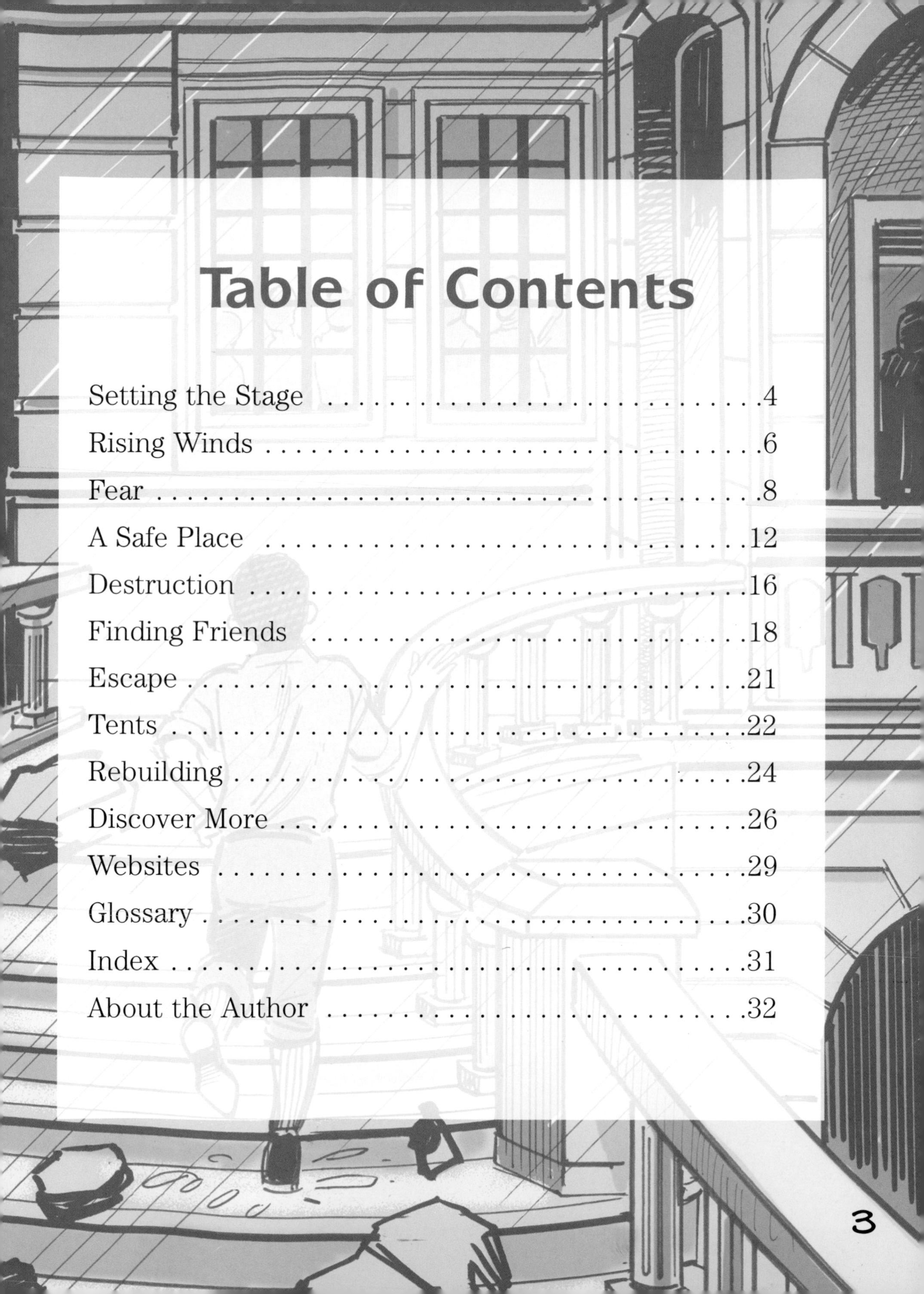

# Table of Contents

Setting the Stage . . . . . . . . . . . . . . . . . . . . . . . . . . . . .4

Rising Winds . . . . . . . . . . . . . . . . . . . . . . . . . . . . . . .6

Fear . . . . . . . . . . . . . . . . . . . . . . . . . . . . . . . . . . . . .8

A Safe Place . . . . . . . . . . . . . . . . . . . . . . . . . . . . . .12

Destruction . . . . . . . . . . . . . . . . . . . . . . . . . . . . . . .16

Finding Friends . . . . . . . . . . . . . . . . . . . . . . . . . . . .18

Escape . . . . . . . . . . . . . . . . . . . . . . . . . . . . . . . . . .21

Tents . . . . . . . . . . . . . . . . . . . . . . . . . . . . . . . . . . .22

Rebuilding . . . . . . . . . . . . . . . . . . . . . . . . . . . . . . .24

Discover More . . . . . . . . . . . . . . . . . . . . . . . . . . . . .26

Websites . . . . . . . . . . . . . . . . . . . . . . . . . . . . . . . . .29

Glossary . . . . . . . . . . . . . . . . . . . . . . . . . . . . . . . . .30

Index . . . . . . . . . . . . . . . . . . . . . . . . . . . . . . . . . . .31

About the Author . . . . . . . . . . . . . . . . . . . . . . . . . . .32

# The Galveston County Daily News

Tuesday

Issue 2  Volume 3

September 15, 1900

## Night of Terror Leaves Thousands Dead or Stranded

Last week's hurricane struck with enormous force. Winds far stronger than the Weather Service had predicted swept bathers from the beach out to sea. Volunteers, working under the direction of the Red Cross, are trying to help families identify the wounded and the dead. Numbers are still coming in, but it is estimated that as many as 10,000 people may have died. Among these are all the girls from the orphanage. It is believed that none of them has survived.

Thousands have been stranded since their homes collapsed. Government and business buildings across the island lie in ruin. Work teams have begun to clear away the rubble, as the city remains in shock.

On September 8, 1900, a hurricane hit Galveston, Texas that changed the city and its residents forever. At the turn of the century, Galveston was one of the wealthiest cities in the United States. By the end of the horrific storm, it was almost unrecognizable with overwhelming damage and destruction throughout.

On the morning of September 8, winds began to pick up with great intensity and massive ocean waves crashed on the beaches.

*"I'm glad I'se living," is a statement many expressed, including this boy, in the aftermath of the Galveston hurricane in 1900.*

By the end of the day, it is estimated that winds reached close to 130 miles per hour, the majority of the city was destroyed, and one-sixth of the population of Galveston was killed. One of the saddest stories from the storm occurred at St. Mary's orphanage. All but three of the children living there were killed, along with the nuns who were their caretakers.

Galveston prides itself on rebuilding rather quickly. They built a sea wall, but remained vulnerable to future storms. Their economy never completely recovered, and Galveston became a quieter beach town.

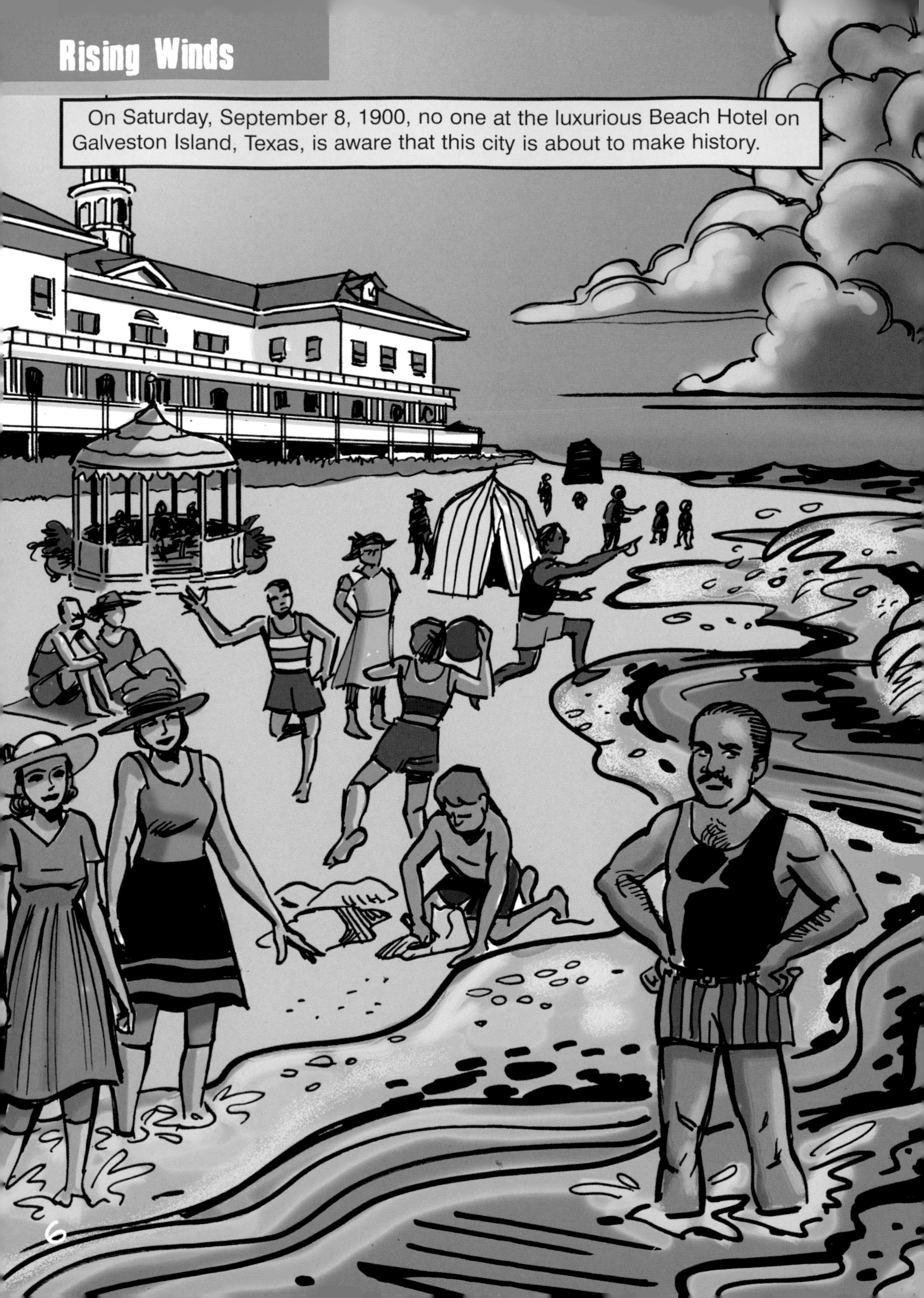
On Saturday, September 8, 1900, no one at the luxurious Beach Hotel on Galveston Island, Texas, is aware that this city is about to make history.

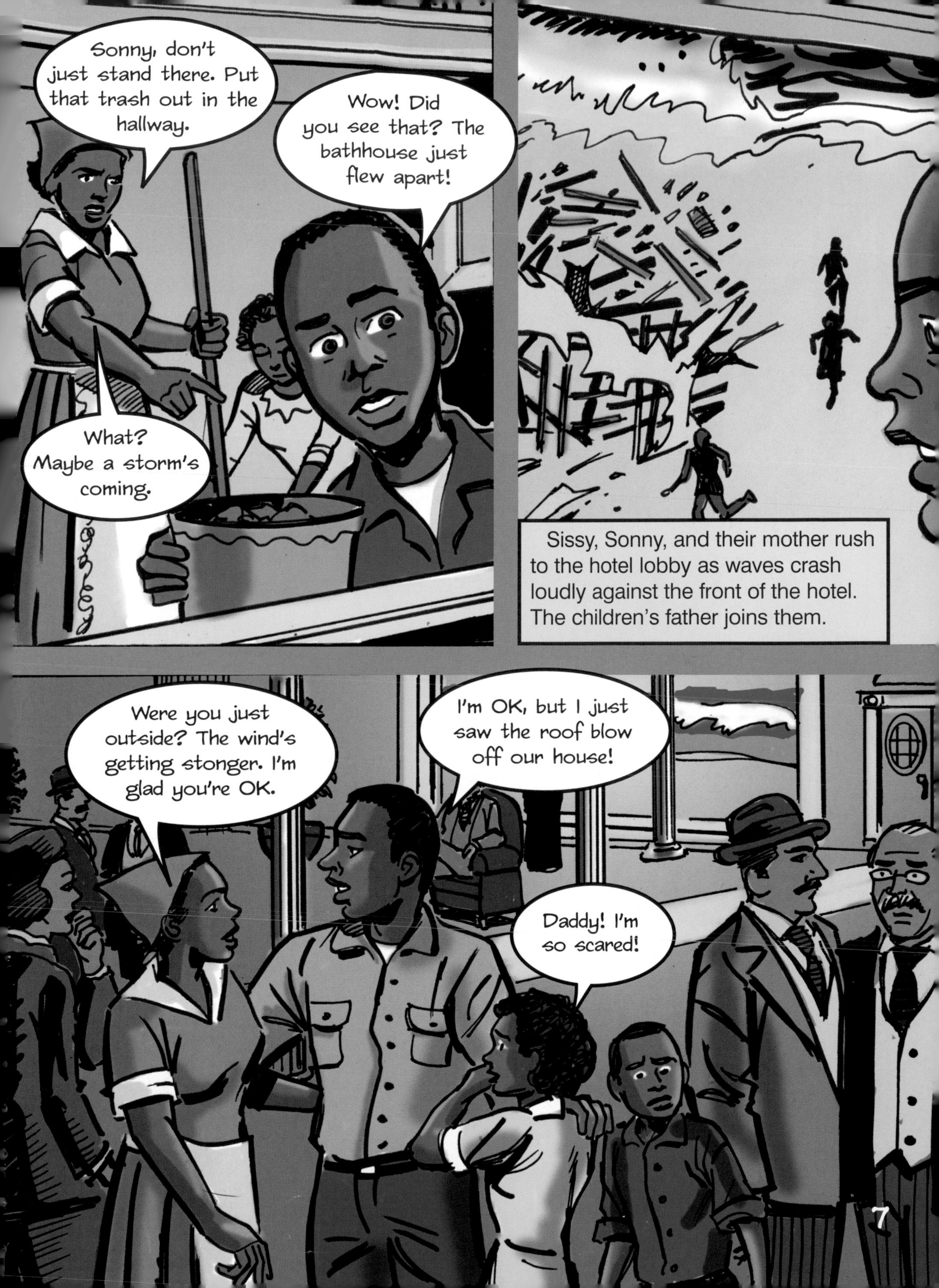

Sonny, don't just stand there. Put that trash out in the hallway.
Wow! Did you see that? The bathhouse just flew apart!
What? Maybe a storm's coming.
Sissy, Sonny, and their mother rush to the hotel lobby as waves crash loudly against the front of the hotel. The children's father joins them.
Were you just outside? The wind's getting stonger. I'm glad you're OK.
I'm OK, but I just saw the roof blow off our house!
Daddy! I'm so scared!

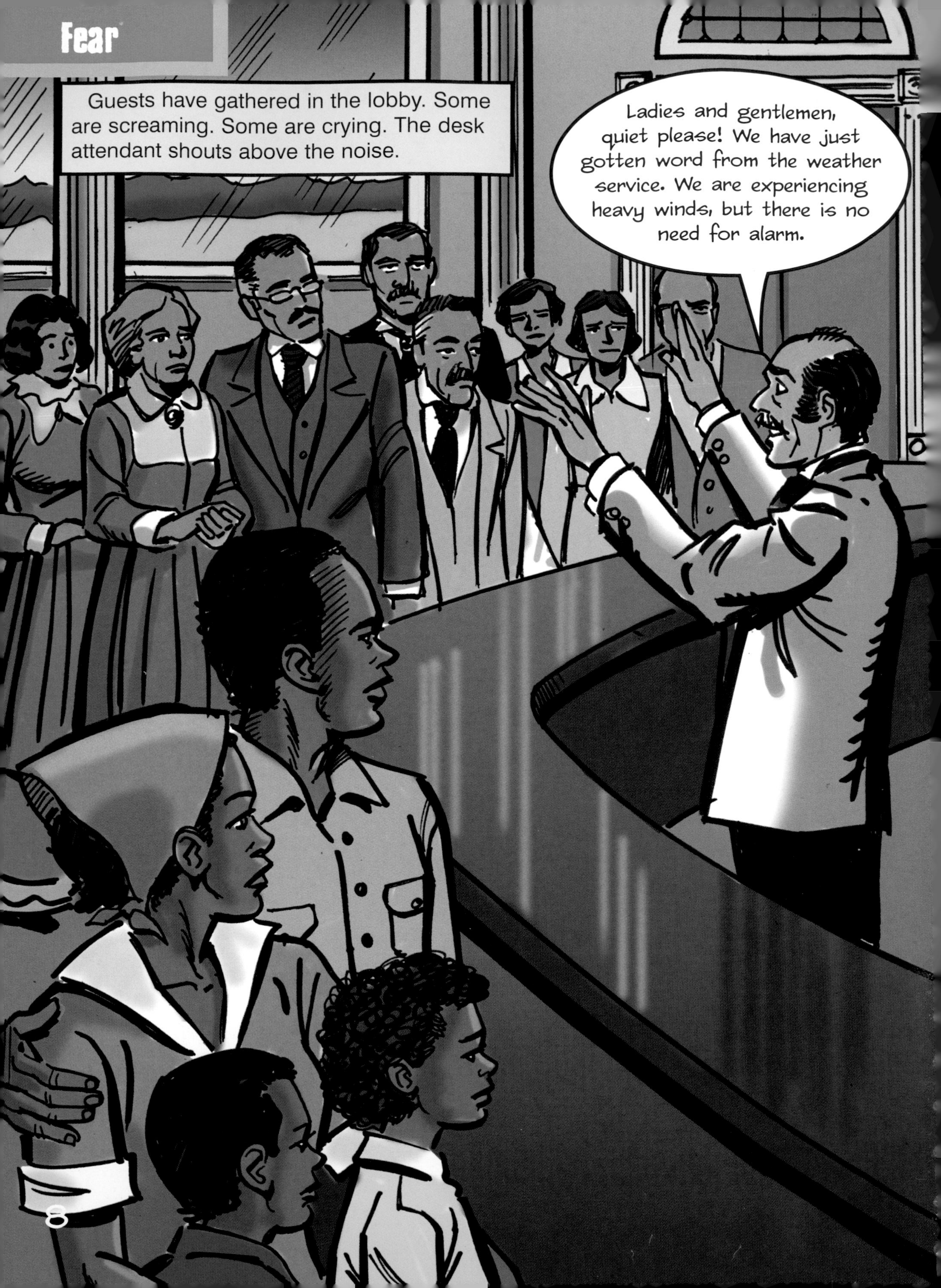
Guests have gathered in the lobby. Some are screaming. Some are crying. The desk attendant shouts above the noise.
Ladies and gentlemen, quiet please! We have just gotten word from the weather service. We are experiencing heavy winds, but there is no need for alarm.

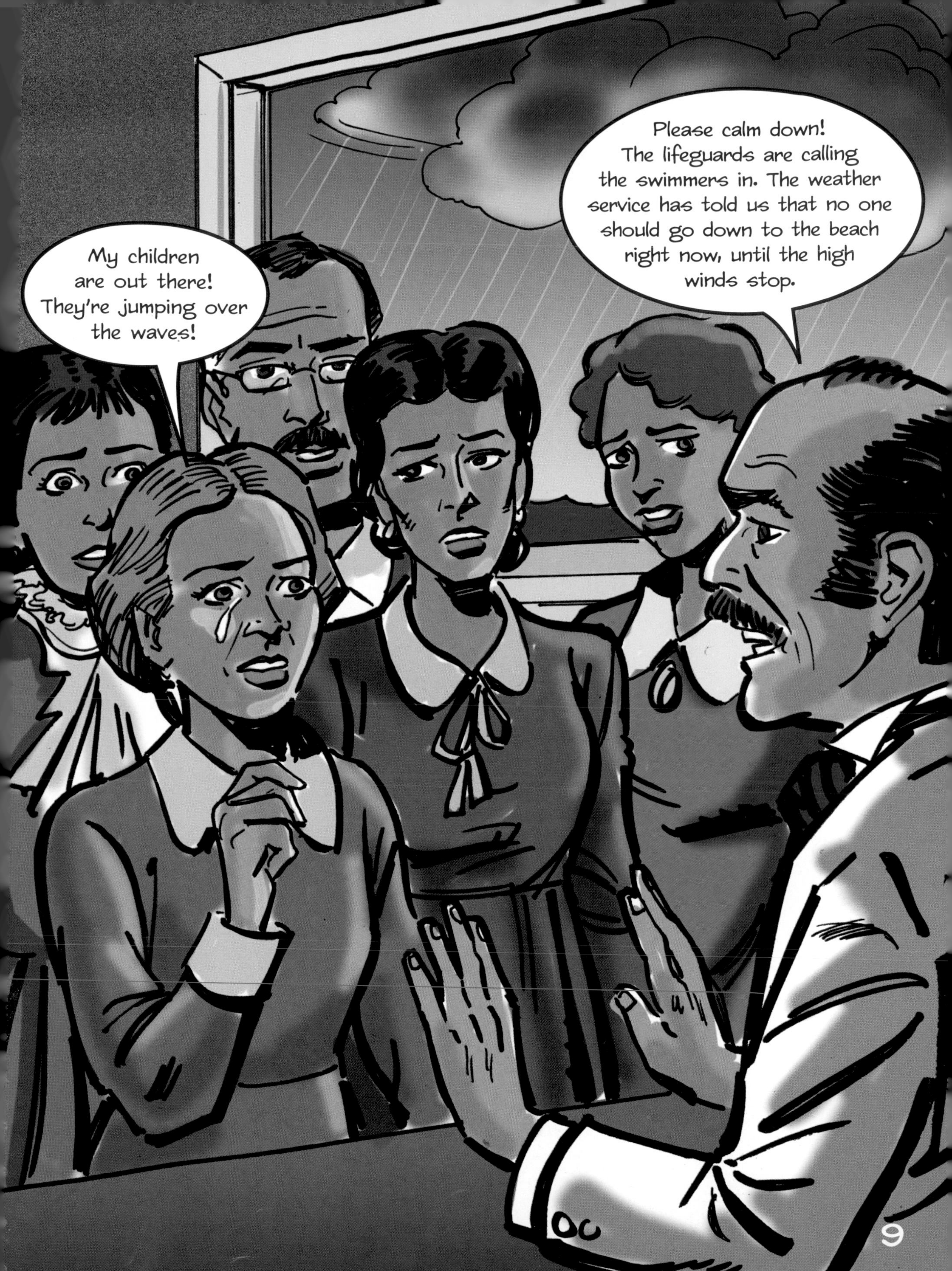
My children are out there! They're jumping over the waves!
Please calm down! The lifeguards are calling the swimmers in. The weather service has told us that no one should go down to the beach right now, until the high winds stop.

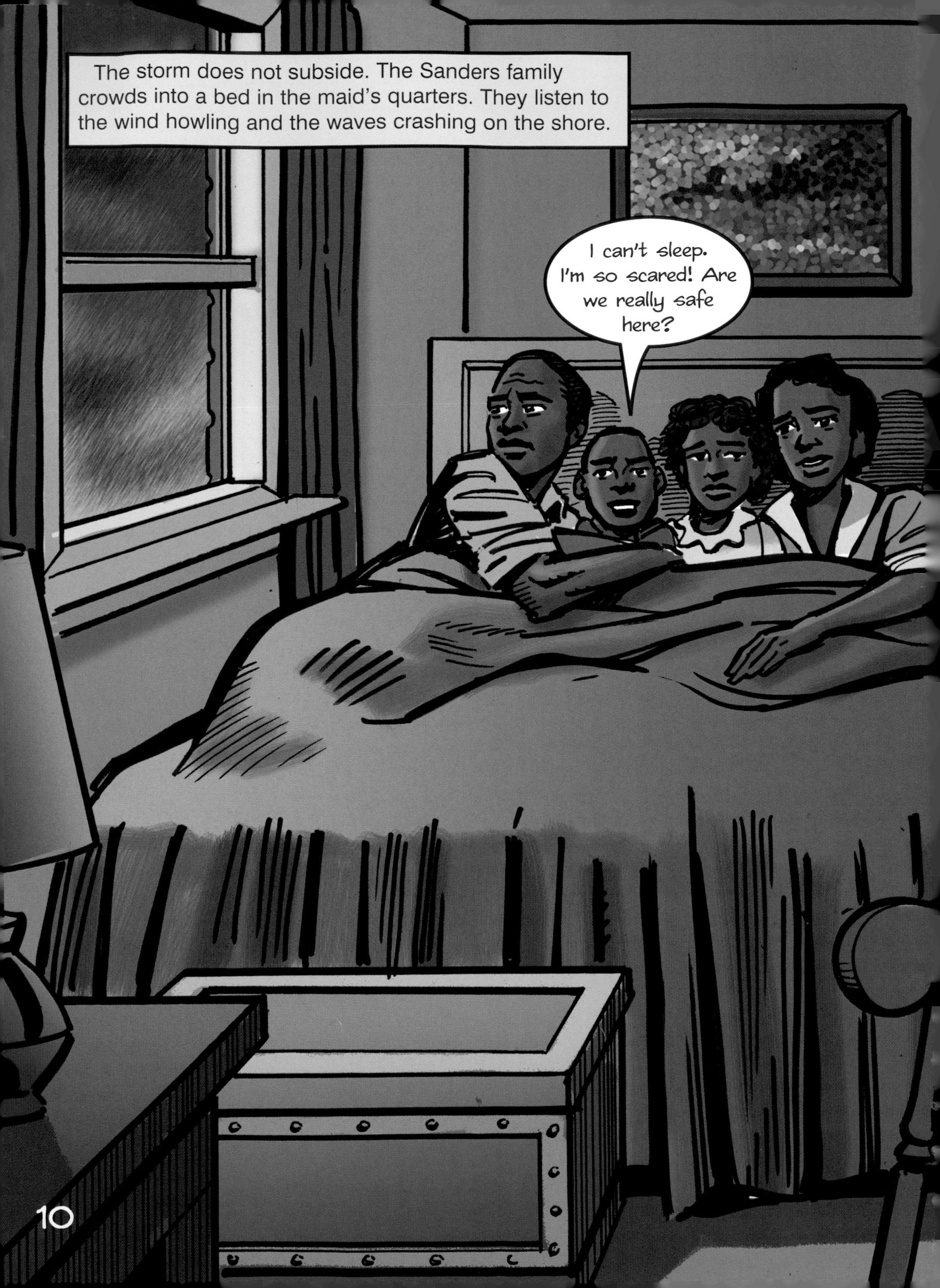
The storm does not subside. The Sanders family crowds into a bed in the maid's quarters. They listen to the wind howling and the waves crashing on the shore.
I can't sleep. I'm so scared! Are we really safe here?

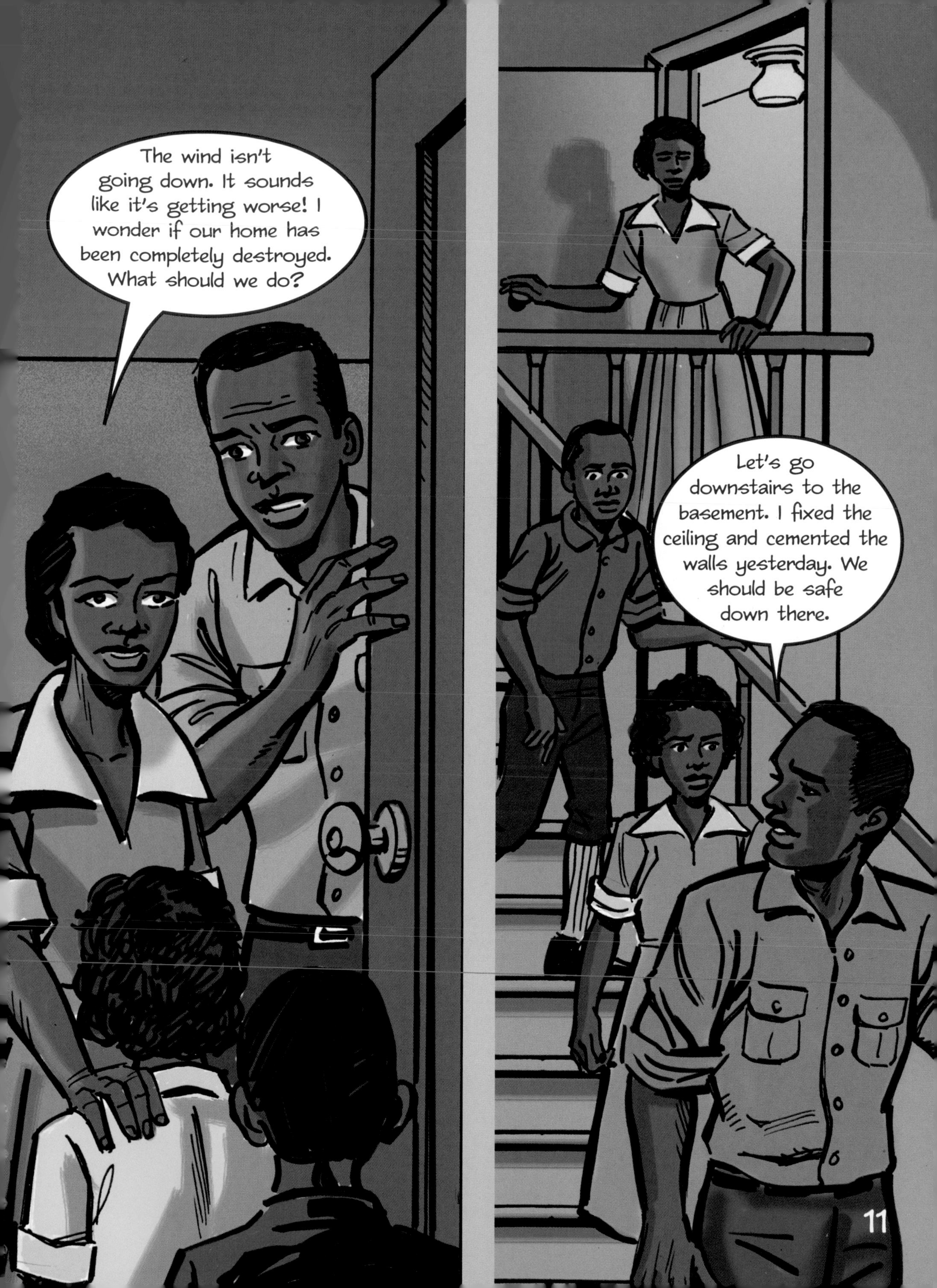
The wind isn't going down. It sounds like it's getting worse! I wonder if our home has been completely destroyed. What should we do?
Let's go downstairs to the basement. I fixed the ceiling and cemented the walls yesterday. We should be safe down there.

# A Safe Place

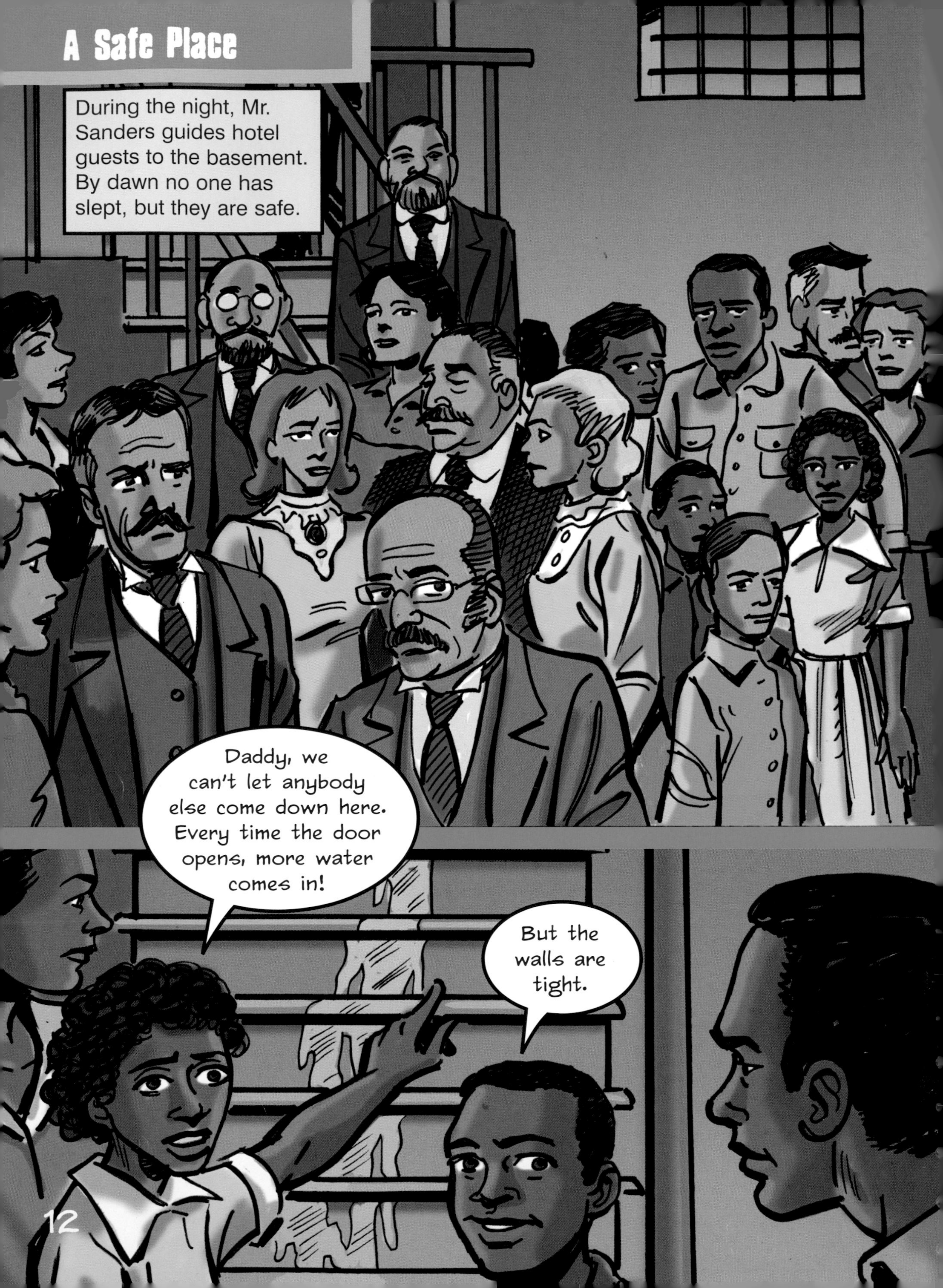
During the night, Mr. Sanders guides hotel guests to the basement. By dawn no one has slept, but they are safe.
Daddy, we can't let anybody else come down here. Every time the door opens, more water comes in!
But the walls are tight.

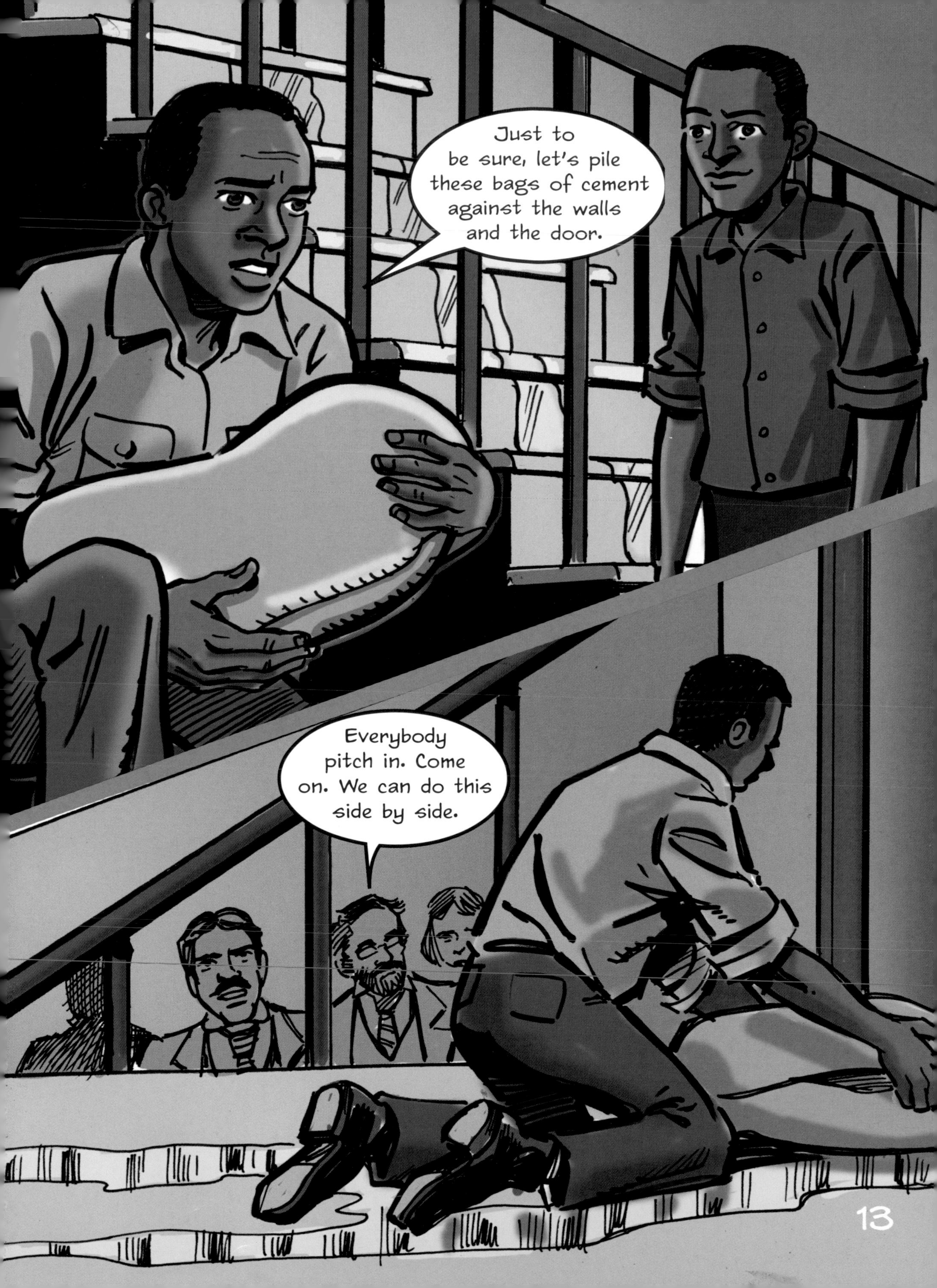
Just to be sure, let's pile these bags of cement against the walls and the door.
Everybody pitch in. Come on. We can do this side by side.

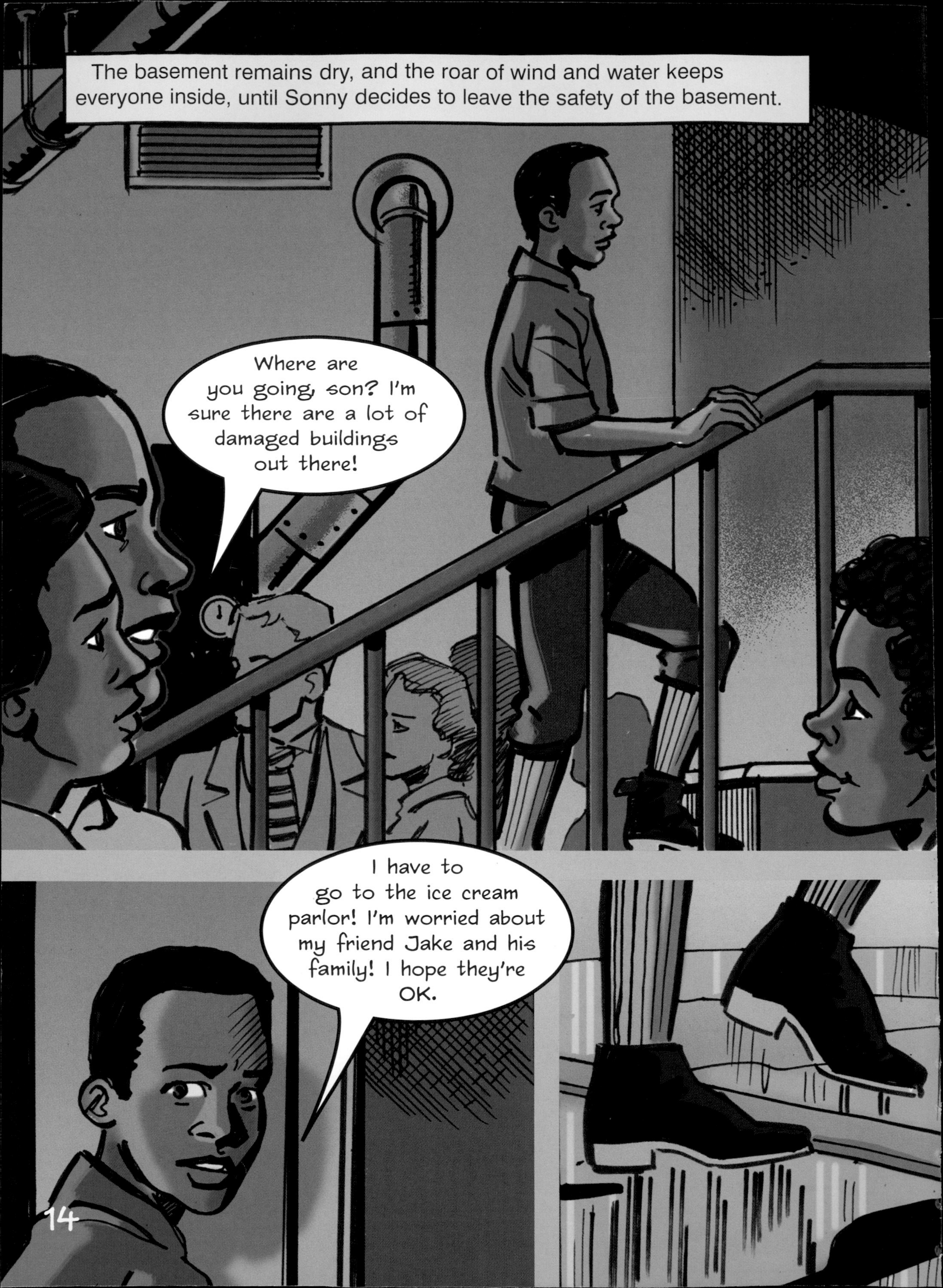
The basement remains dry, and the roar of wind and water keeps everyone inside, until Sonny decides to leave the safety of the basement.
Where are you going, son? I'm sure there are a lot of damaged buildings out there!
I have to go to the ice cream parlor! I'm worried about my friend Jake and his family! I hope they're OK.

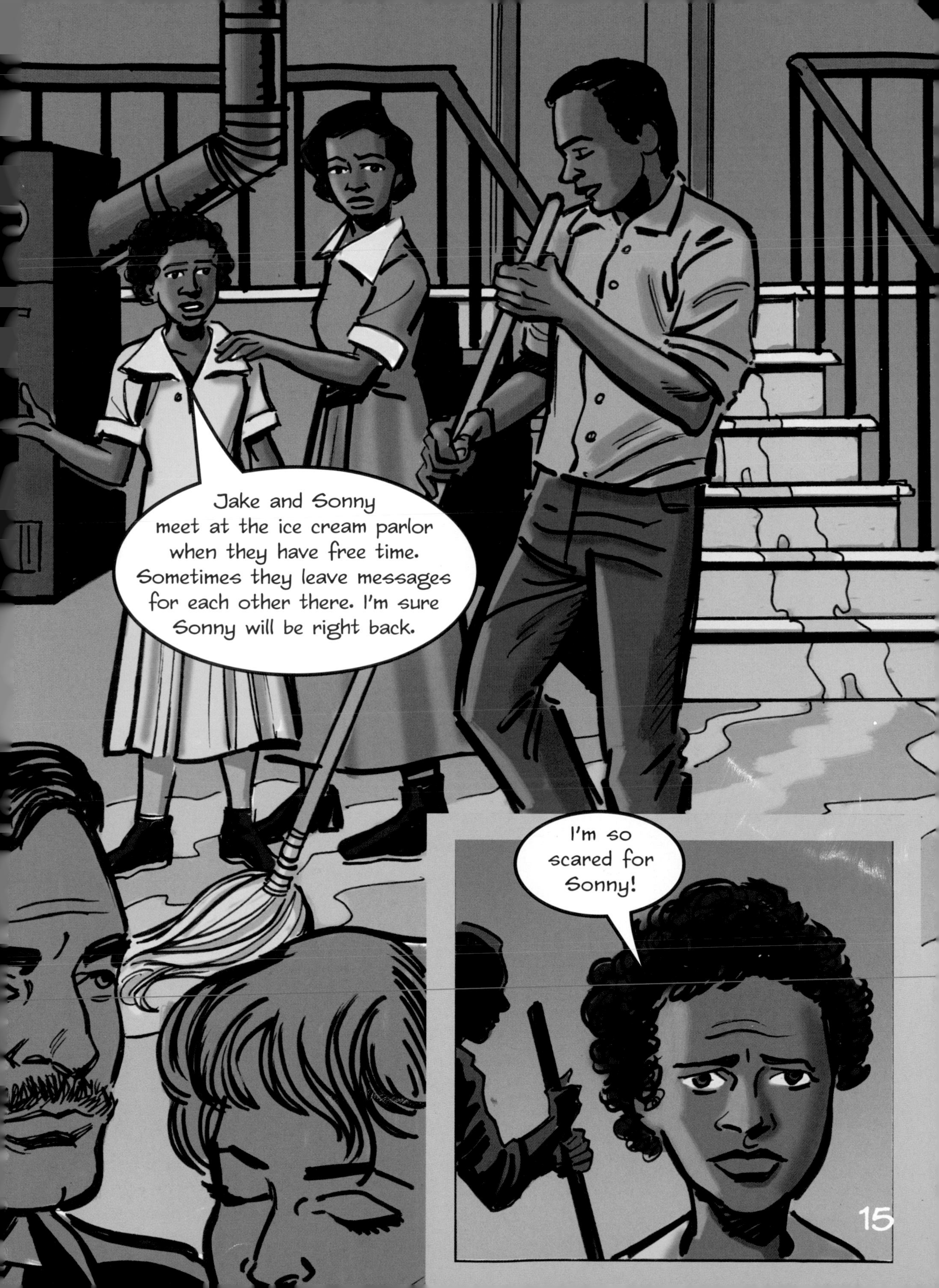
Jake and Sonny meet at the ice cream parlor when they have free time. Sometimes they leave messages for each other there. I'm sure Sonny will be right back.
I'm so scared for Sonny!

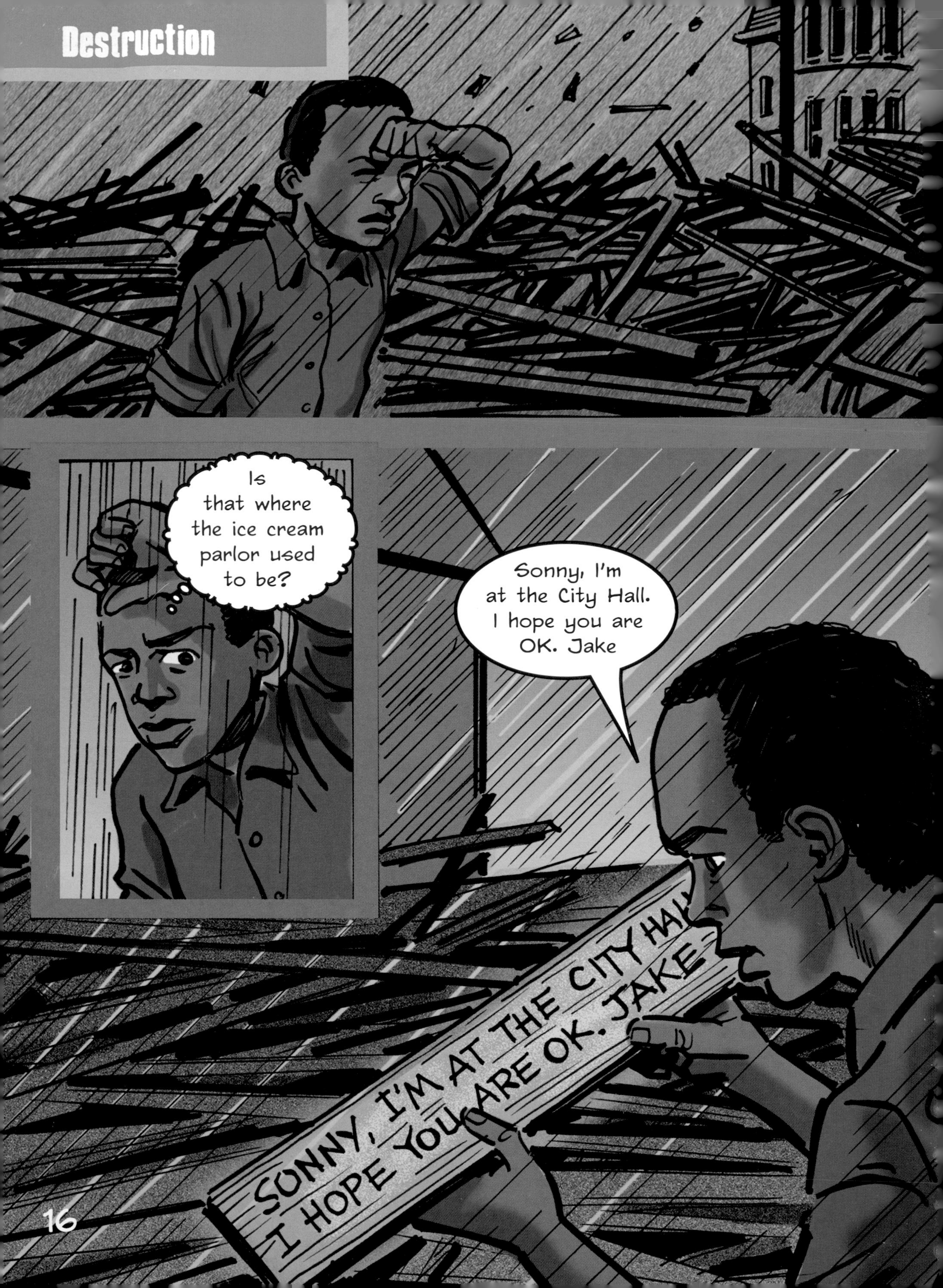
Is that where the ice cream parlor used to be?
Sonny, I'm at the City Hall. I hope you are OK. Jake
SONNY, I'M AT THE CITY HAL
I HOPE YOU ARE OK. JAKE

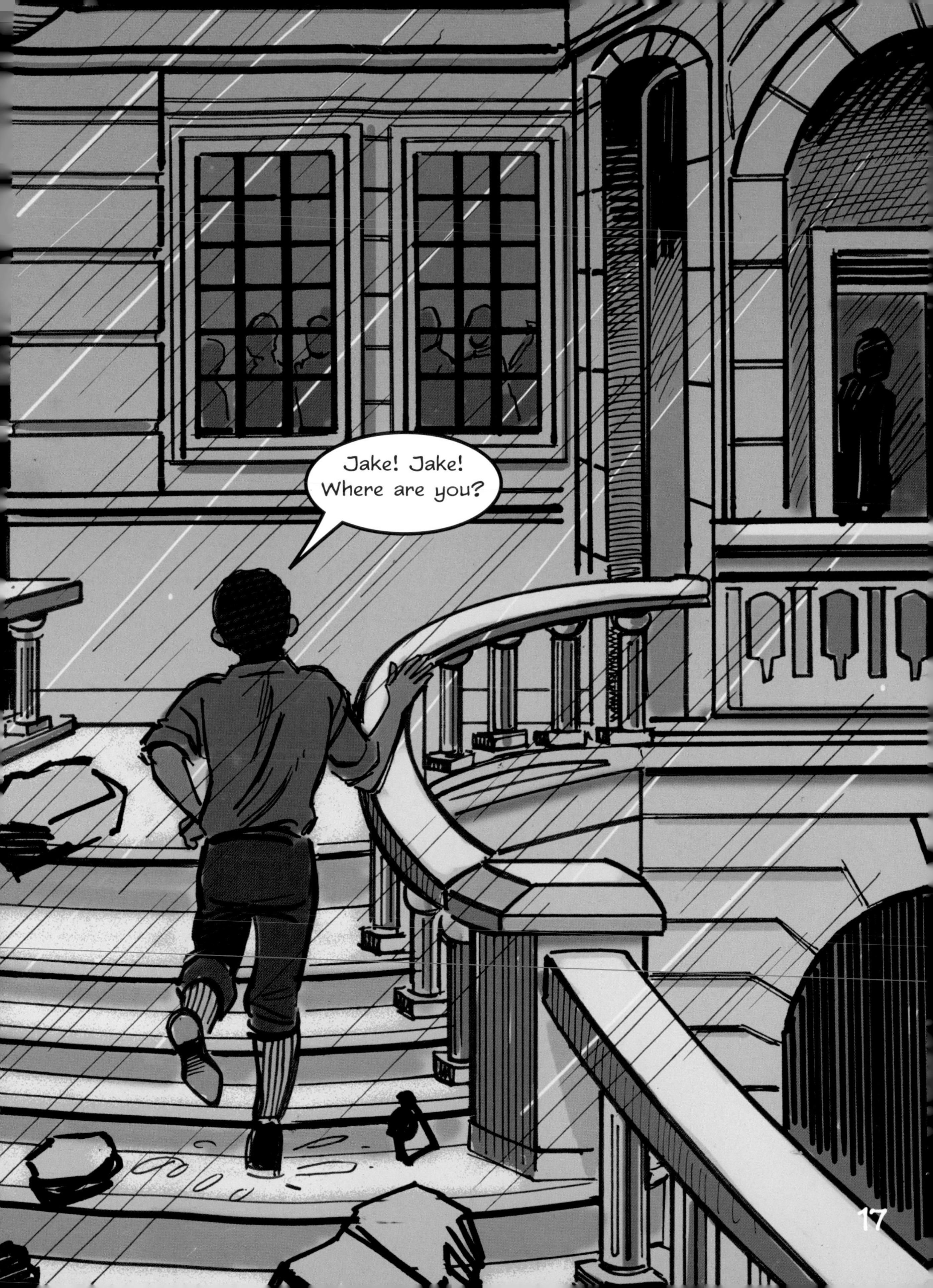
Jake! Jake! Where are you?

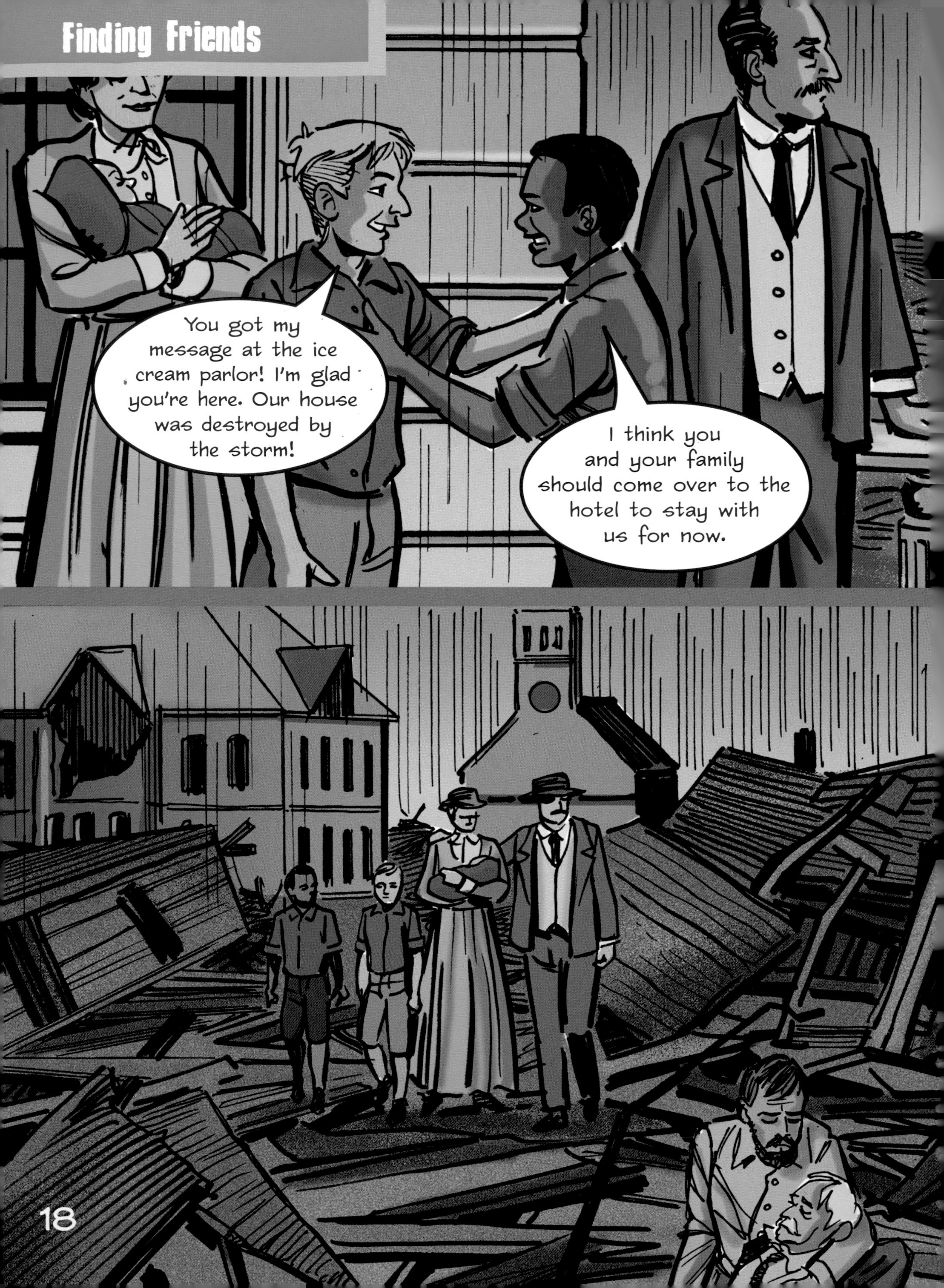
You got my message at the ice cream parlor! I'm glad you're here. Our house was destroyed by the storm!
I think you and your family should come over to the hotel to stay with us for now.

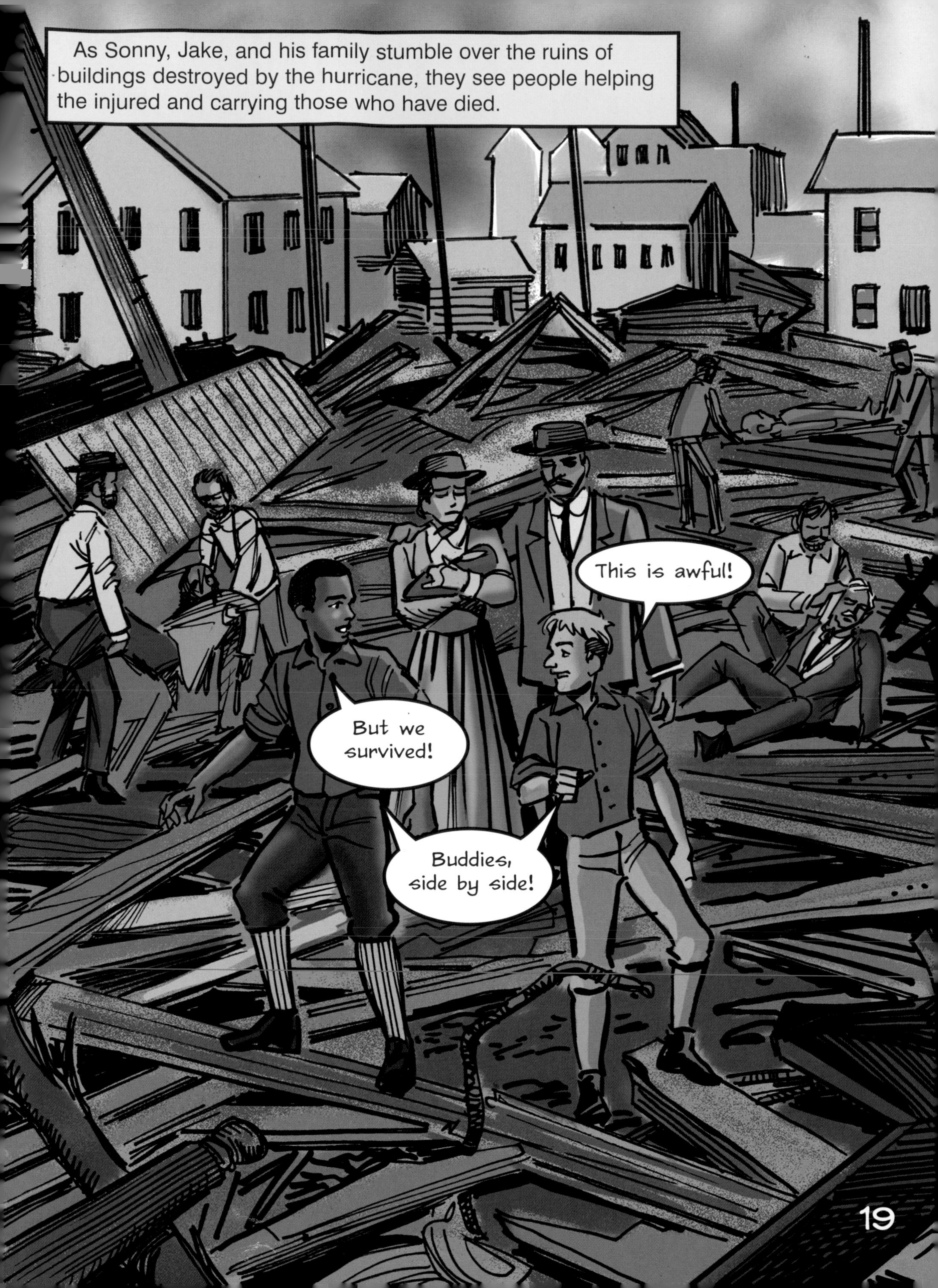
As Sonny, Jake, and his family stumble over the ruins of buildings destroyed by the hurricane, they see people helping the injured and carrying those who have died.
This is awful!
But we survived!
Buddies, side by side!

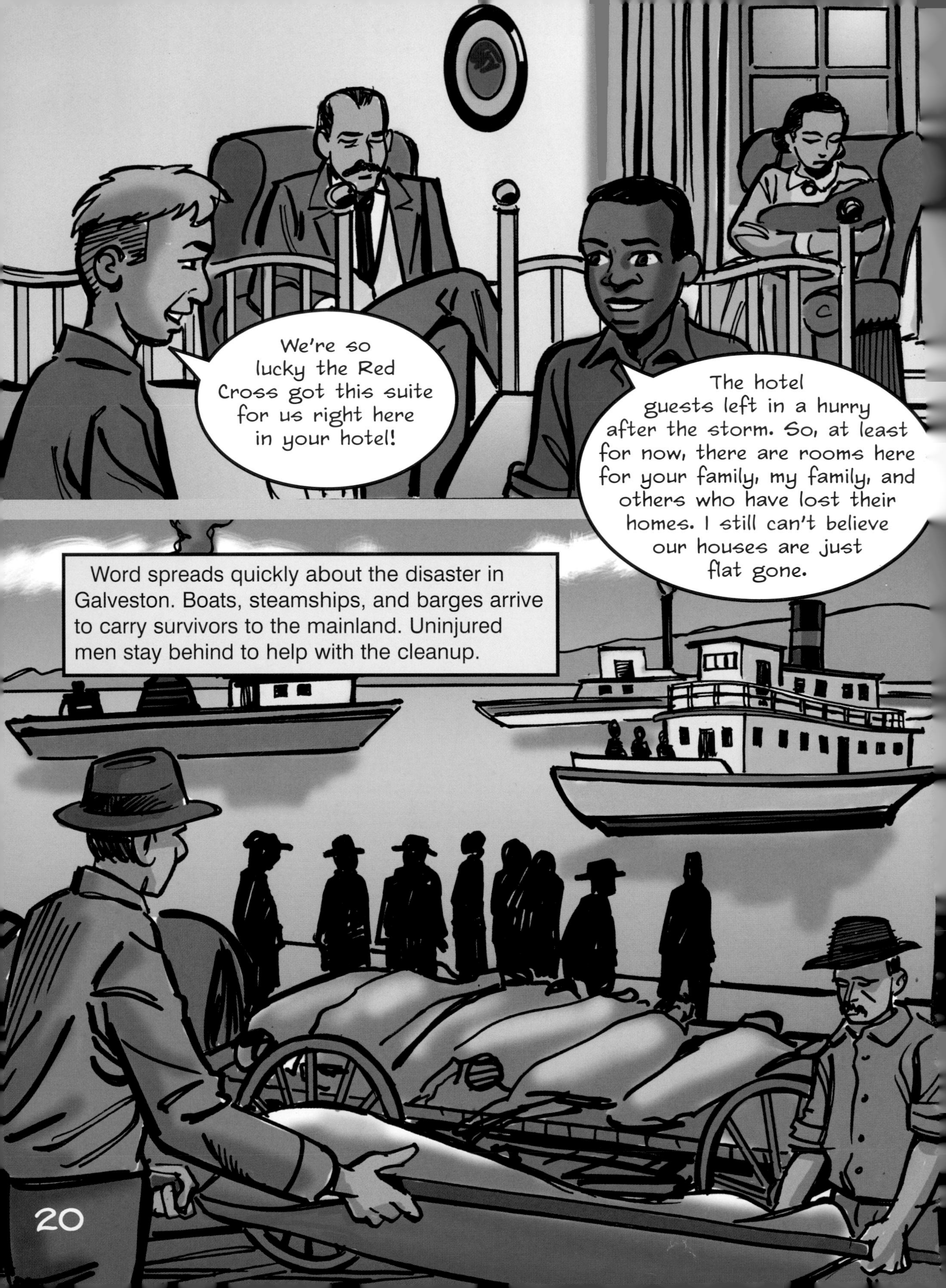
We're so lucky the Red Cross got this suite for us right here in your hotel!
The hotel guests left in a hurry after the storm. So, at least for now, there are rooms here for your family, my family, and others who have lost their homes. I still can't believe our houses are just flat gone.
Word spreads quickly about the disaster in Galveston. Boats, steamships, and barges arrive to carry survivors to the mainland. Uninjured men stay behind to help with the cleanup.

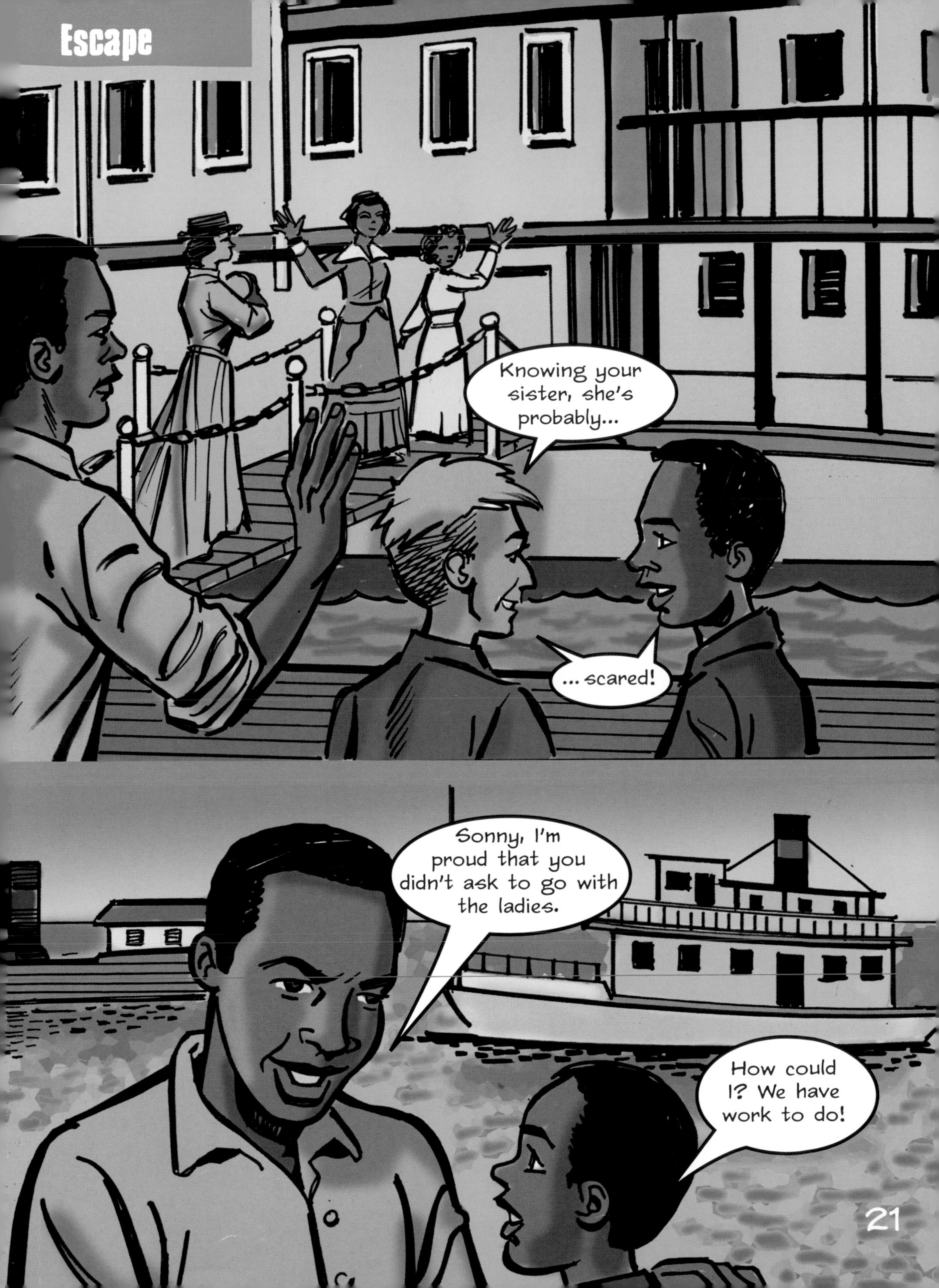
Knowing your sister, she's probably...
... scared!
Sonny, I'm proud that you didn't ask to go with the ladies.
How could I? We have work to do!

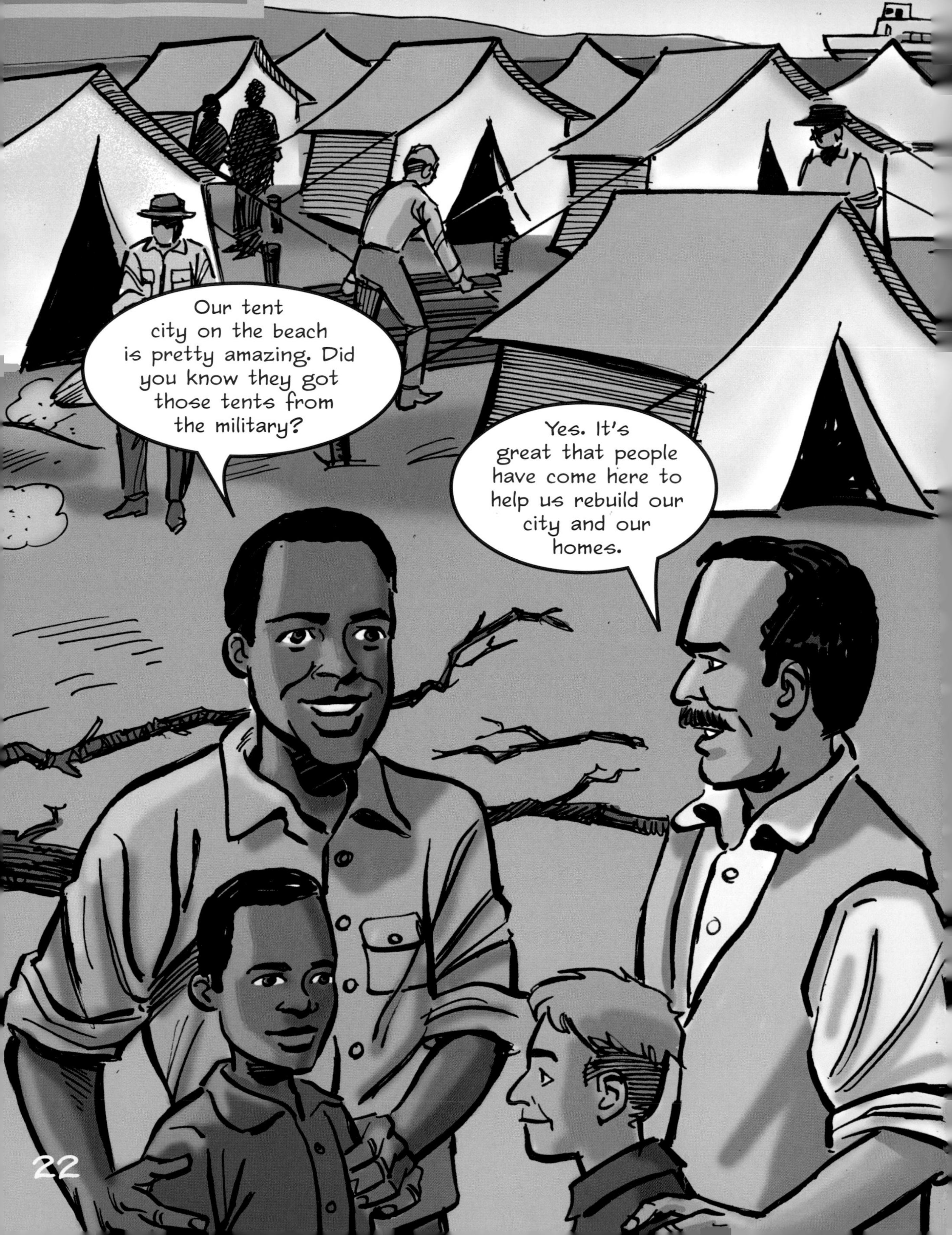
Our tent city on the beach is pretty amazing. Did you know they got those tents from the military?
Yes. It's great that people have come here to help us rebuild our city and our homes.

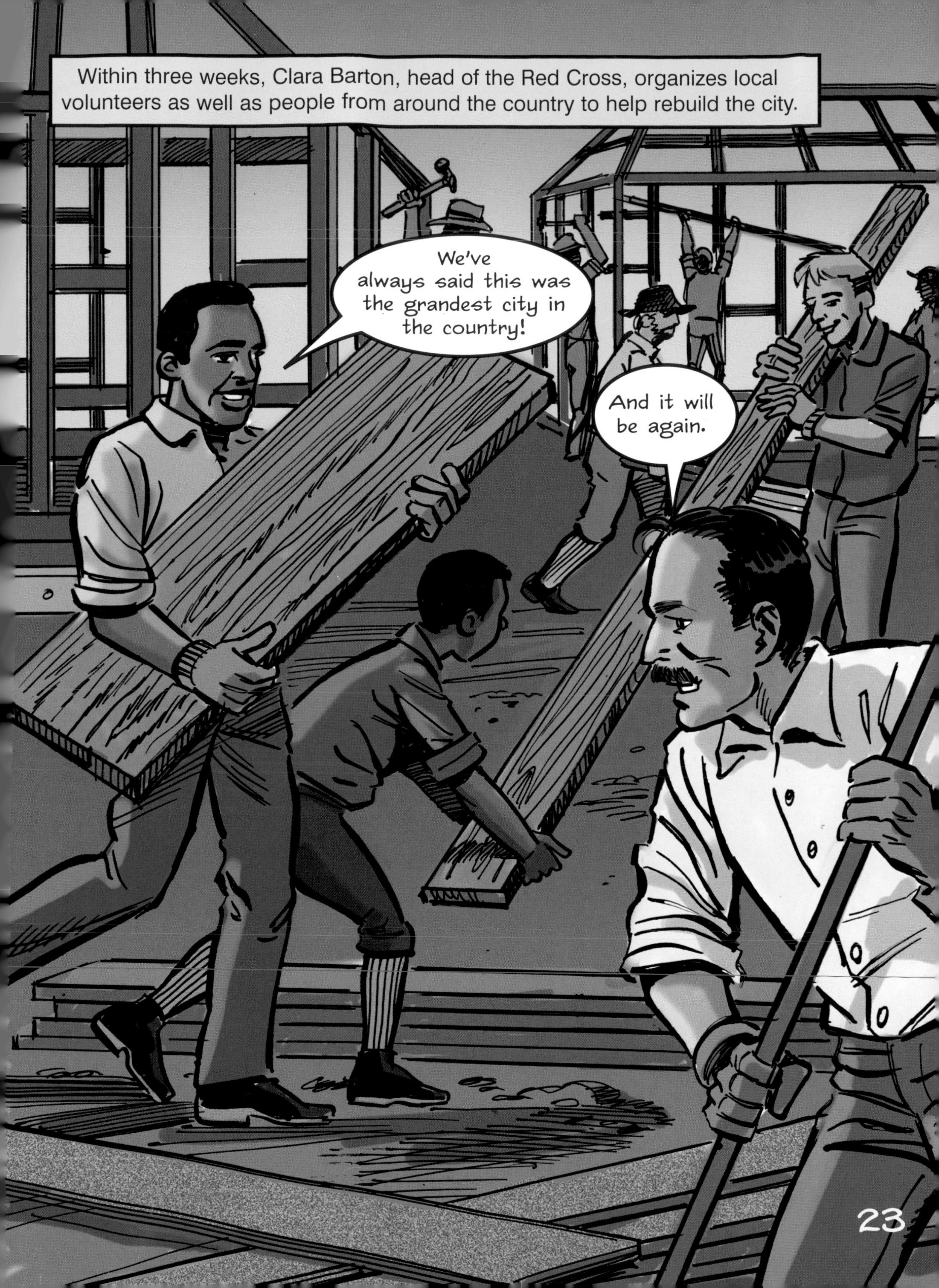
Within three weeks, Clara Barton, head of the Red Cross, organizes local volunteers as well as people from around the country to help rebuild the city.
We've always said this was the grandest city in the country!
And it will be again.

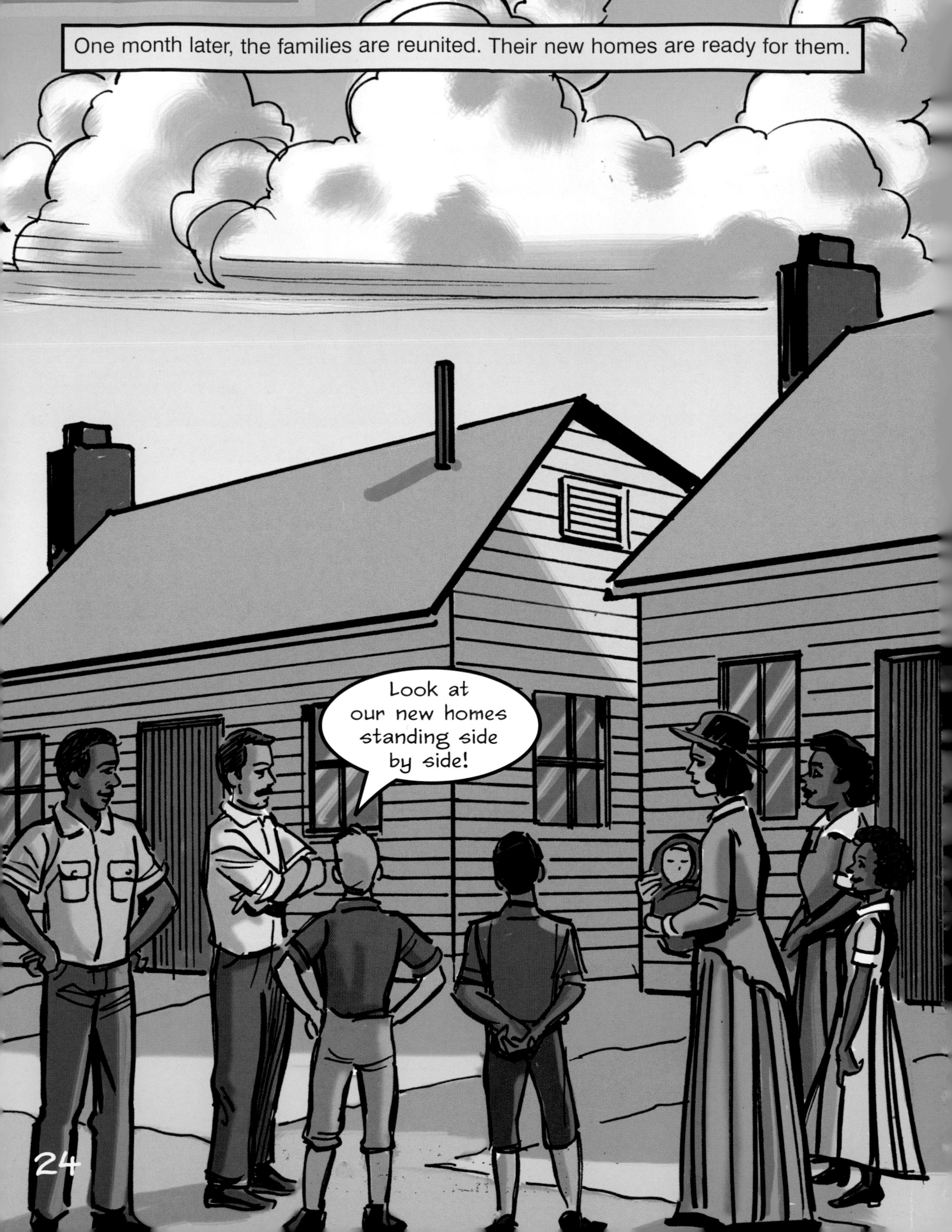
One month later, the families are reunited. Their new homes are ready for them.
Look at our new homes standing side by side!

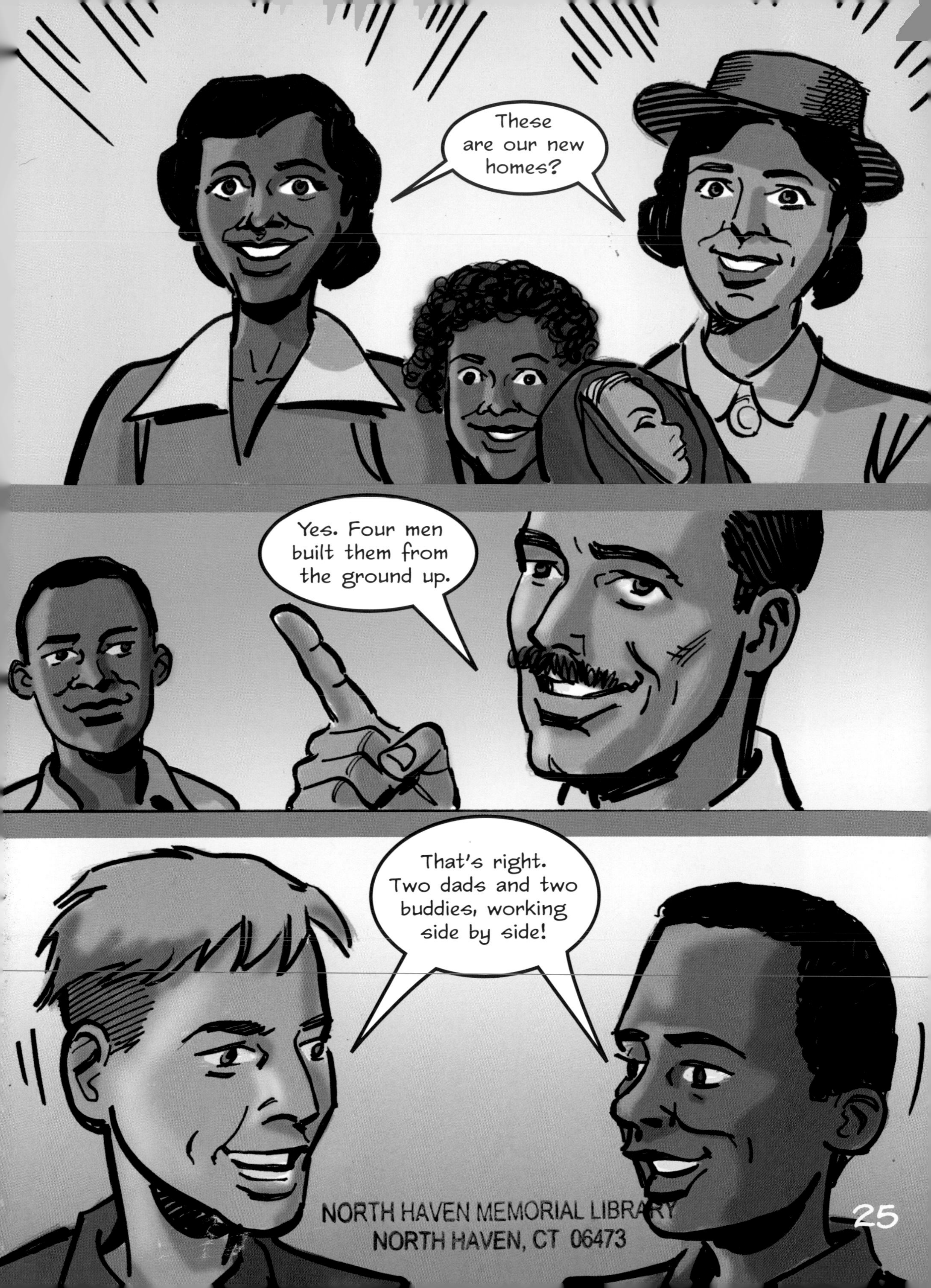
These are our new homes?
Yes. Four men built them from the ground up.
That's right. Two dads and two buddies, working side by side!

## How many died in the Galveston Hurricane of 1900?

An estimated 8,000 to 12,000 lives were lost. This was more than the amount lost in the San Francisco Earthquake and the Great Chicago Fire combined. Some people drowned. Some were crushed by falling buildings. Some were stranded and died of starvation.

*Many who died remained in their homes which crushed them as the wooden structures were pummeled by the winds and rain.*

## Why didn't people leave before the storm came?

When the Weather Service notified the Galveston station of the approaching storm, forecasters considered it just another spell of high winds that often spread across the island. In fact, jumping through breaking waves was a tourist attraction. Initially, officials were so unconcerned that no effort was made to clear the beaches. Most of the swimmers on the beach the morning of September 8, 1900, were washed out to sea or dashed to the ground, as a five-foot wall of water pounded the shore.

## How quickly did help arrive?

Clara Barton, head of the Red Cross, responded immediately. In less than a week, the 76-year-old had made a nationwide call for assistance and was handling operations at the Galveston headquarters in person. She organized the efforts of the rich and the poor, city officials, and volunteers. Together they carried away the dead, helped the wounded, and cleared the debris.

*Clara Barton was instrumental in getting Galveston back on its feet after the hurricane.*

*Tent cities along the shore served as temporary shelters during the period of rebuilding.*

## Was the city rebuilt?

Fifteen acres had been swept clean by the storm. At least 3,600 elegant homes were destroyed. At first, many believed the city was gone forever, but then a wave of determination to revive the city spread among the survivors. Damaged structures were repaired, such as the City Hall, the Opera House, many churches, and hotels. New homes were erected on land where miles of debris were removed.

City leaders learned that day that heavy winds in the area should not be taken lightly. To protect the city, they built a 17-foot granite wall between the ocean and the city. Completed in 1910, it required 11,000,000 pounds (5,000,000 kilograms) of filling to construct. Galveston had risen again and was protected.

The Galveston hurricane of 1900 was one of the most disastrous hurricanes in U.S. history, but the city is once again a vital community.

*Very few houses were left untouched, but the citizens did not give up, and rebuilding began soon after the winds died down.*

## Have There Been Other Hurricanes?

The hurricane from 1900 remains the deadliest, but Galveston has been victim to other intense storms since then. In 1915, a hurricane slammed into the city, killing 275 people. In 1983, Hurricane Alicia came ashore causing a great deal of damage. In 2008, Hurricane Ike proved to be extremely destructive, with thousands requiring rescue and billions of dollars worth of damage.

In 1954, the World Meteorological Organization discovered hurricanes are easier to track when given names. A list is compiled in alphabetical order and names are recycled every six years. If a hurricane is especially destructive, the name is retired and another name replaces it. Recently, the name Ike was retired, and Isaias has taken its place.

# Websites

www.1900storm.com

www.qsl.net/w5www/hurricane.html

www.dallasnews.com/sharedcontent/dws/spe/2005/1900

www.history.noaa.gov/stories_tales/cline2.html

www.cnn.com/SPECIALS/2000/galveston

# Glossary

**debris** (duh-BREE): Debris is made up of scattered pieces of buildings and other objects after they have been blow apart or destroyed.

**determination** (di-tur-min-AY-shun): When people make up their minds to fix something even when the job is very hard, they have determination.

**disastrous** (duh-ZASS-trus): If something is disastrous, it is very harmful.

**erect** (i-REKT): To erect a house is to build it.

**granite** (GRAN-it): Granite is hard, gray rock. A granite wall is very strong.

**headquarters** (HED-kwor-turz): A headquarters is the place where operations are organized. People meet at the headquarters to get directions for their work on a project.

**luxurious** (luhk-SHUH-ree-us): A luxurious hotel is beautiful and expensive.

**reunite** (ree-yoo-NITE): When people reunite, they get back together again.

**starvation** (star-VAY-shuhn): A person who has no food may die of starvation.

**stranded** (STRAND-id): If people are stranded, they are stuck and cannot get away from a harmful place.

**structure** (STRUHK-chur): A structure is a building.

**tourist attraction** (TOOR-ist uh-TRAK-shuhn): A tourist attraction is a place where people go to visit for vacations and fun.

**vital** (VYE-tuhl): A vital city is one with lots of activity. It is full of life.

**volunteer** (vol-uhn-TIHR): A volunteer works for no pay.

# Index

Barton, Clara    23, 27

beach(es)    9, 22, 26

Beach Hotel    6

City Hall    16, 28

destroyed    11, 18, 19, 28

disaster    20

hurricane(s)    5, 19, 28

tent city    22

water    12, 14, 26

# About the Author

Jo Cleland, Professor Emeritus of Reading Education, taught in the College of Education at Arizona State University West for 11 years, preparing future teachers for classroom experience and guiding graduate students to refine their skills. Prior to entering university teaching, Jo spent 20 years in public education and continues to work with children through her storytelling and workshops. She has presented to audiences of teachers across the nation and the world, bringing to all her favorite message: **What we learn with delight, we never forget**.

# About the Illustrator

Pete McDonnell is an illustrator who has worked in his field for twenty-four years. He has been creating comics, storyboards, and pop-art style illustration for clients such as Marvel Comics, the History Channel, Microsoft, Nestle, Sega, and many more. He lives in Sonoma County, California with his wife Shannon (also an illustrator) and son Jacob.